THE CRUSADES

A History from Beginning to End

Copyright © 2017 by Hourly History.

All rights reserved.

Table of Contents

Introduction
Peace in War: A Background to the Crusades
The First Crusade
Establishing the Crusader States
The Second Crusade
The Third Crusade
The Fourth Crusade
The Children's Crusade and Crusading Against Christians
The Fifth and Sixth Crusades
The Seventh and Eighth Crusades
The Last Crusade
Conclusion

Introduction

One place cuts through all of the complexities of the outbreak of the extended Holy War to represent the fundamental disagreement between Christians and Muslims—Jerusalem. Jerusalem is the very cornerstone of over a millennium of contention between Christians and Muslims, with each religion believing themselves to be its true and rightful owner. For Christians, Jerusalem is supremely sacred as the site of the Crucifixion, Resurrection, and Ascension of Jesus Christ. Jerusalem is equally sacred to Muslims who believe their Prophet Muhammad, founder of the Islamic faith, experienced his own Night Journey and Ascension on this land.

In the year 638 CE, the Caliph Omar, direct successor to the Prophet Muhammad, captured Jerusalem from the ancient Christians who ruled it. For a few centuries, the two religions coexisted reasonably peacefully. Muslims did not forcibly convert Christians to their faith, nor did they close churches or ban Christian worship, but they did assert their authority as the ruling power in the land. Christians were forbidden from preaching in the presence of Muslims or criticizing the Muslim faith in any way under the penalty of death. As a result, few Christians dared make the pilgrimage.

The uneasy coexistence of Christians and Muslims in the Holy Land was disrupted at the beginning of the second millennium with seismic changes taking place on both sides of the religious divide. During his lifetime, the Prophet Muhammad had not only founded the religion of Islam but had united much of what was then termed Arabia into a single entity. As with any flourishing society, Islam wanted to expand its influence and conquered the Middle East, much of Central Asia, northwest India, North Africa, southern Italy, and parts of modern-day Greece.

In parts of the Islamic Empire where Christians and Muslims lived in close proximity, a truce was upheld, yet the balance of power between the two sides was far too delicate to last. In an attempt to rein in the spread of Islam and claim ownership of the Holy Land, the Christian west launched a military campaign like no other. This time, fighting men did not receive the usual call to arms to defend their country. Instead, they received a call to the cross to defend their god. Offering the prize of guaranteed redemption at the gates of heaven, papal authorities inspired a religious zeal in their men that could not be extinguished.

While the First and Fourth Crusades could reasonably be described as successful, the majority of the other seven crusading expeditions to the Muslim east ended with disaster. Over two centuries, repeated attempts to reclaim the Holy Land of Jerusalem ended in failure and yet, again and again, ordinary people took the cross and made the arduous journey east. In launching their Holy War and maintaining its momentum over two centuries, the Crusaders showed the world the devastating effect of forcibly dividing the world along the lines of religion.

Chapter One

Peace in War: A Background to the Crusades

"Dues le Volt! (God wills it!)"

—The first Crusaders

In the mid-eleventh century, western Europe entered a period of massive transformation. The population across the mostly feudal, inter-connected, and yet far from civilized collection of kingdoms was booming. Economic prosperity followed as sea-faring Italians revolutionized European trade by pushing back against the Arabs' dominance of the shipping industry. The Norman invasion and conquer of England in 1066 proved that Europeans were capable of mounting formidable military campaigns, and heads of state everywhere were looking for ways of expanding their territory.

The leader of the Seljuk Turks, one of several powerful Muslim tribes, was also hoping to expand his territory. Having successfully overpowered the Abbasid caliphs and taken control of Baghdad, the Seljuks moved on to Anatolia and Byzantine-controlled Armenia. In 1071 the Seljuks destroyed the Byzantine army at the Battle of Manzikert and captured the Byzantine emperor, Romanus IV Diogenes. Now the entire territory of former Christian Asia Minor was vulnerable to Turkish military raids and the gradual migration of Muslim tribes. Next the Seljuks took Antioch in Syria and Nicaea, both huge blows to the Byzantine Empire. By 1095 Islam was knocking on the door of the Byzantine capital of Constantinople and its emperor, Alexius Comnenus, cried out to western Europe for help.

This cry for help came at a significant moment for the Christian powers of western Europe, and how these powers reacted to Emperor Comnenus' cry set the next two centuries of devastating religious war into motion.

Christianity in Europe was entering a stage of revival. The Gregorian reform movement of the eleventh century sought to completely refurbish the structure of the church and bring Christianity back to its purest state. Pope Gregory VII advocated that all bishops, priors, and abbots be canonically-elected by the Pope in Rome. Simony, or the practice of paying for a position in the church, would be abolished and all men of the cloth should return to a state of celibacy. The effect of these reforms on the day-to-day life of the masses was negligible, but the effect on religious life was astounding.

A far-reaching religious revival ensued. Pagans of central and eastern Europe and Scandinavia were swept up in the new fervor for reformed Christianity and converted to Catholicism. The idea of the apocalypse took root, and people began to believe premonitions that the world was soon to come to an end. One popular belief held that the Second Coming of Christ was imminent and that the Last

Emperor, now believed to be the king of the Franks, was waiting to lead the faithful to Jerusalem where they would be taken to heaven. Pilgrimage took on a whole new significance and became a popular way to express extreme piety without the need for a complete lifestyle change. Christians came to see Jerusalem as the destination of their ultimate salvation and resented the fact that the territory was under Muslim rule.

At the end of the eleventh century, Pope Urban II was battling it out with Henry IV, the emperor of Germany, over Gregorian papal reform policies. The Pope wanted complete control over all church appointments while the emperor saw his own authority as supremely divine and opposed all papal reform. Henry IV had gone as far as to appoint an antipope in 1080 and demanded that all citizens under his rule no longer acknowledge Pope Urban II.

Unconcerned, Urban traveled to France in 1095 and invoked the Council of Clermont on November 18 that year. Paradoxically, one of the canons passed during this meeting of ecclesiastical minds was the renewal of the Peace of God, a broad decree intended to limit warfare and protect the vulnerable from harm. A second canon, that of plenary indulgence, undermined the Peace of God. Plenary indulgence planted the idea of crusading into the minds of the masses by promising to grant those who offered assistance to Christians in the east a remission of all penance for sin. Met with a favorable response from his fellow French bishops, Urban took his message out to the people in a great outdoor assembly at Clermont Cathedral. One account of Urban's speech includes the following statement: "Whoever for devotion alone, not to gain honour or money, goes to Jerusalem to liberate the Church of God, can substitute the journey for all penance."

Urban strongly suggested that those people gathered who were not in a state of grace could redeem themselves in God's eyes by fighting to reclaim the Holy City of Jerusalem. The people's response was overwhelming. Knights and peasants alike surged forward crying "Deus le volt" (God wills it), clambering over each other to take possession of a small cross that was to be worn around the neck of every holy warrior. The Crusades were officially underway.

Chapter Two

The First Crusade

"The Crusades—the most signal and most durable monument of human folly that has yet appeared in any age or nation."

—David Hume, *The History of England*

It seems Pope Urban had envisioned a single crusading expedition that, with Bishop Adhemar of Le Puy at its head, would succeed in liberating Jerusalem. However, as word of his holy call to arms spread, the Crusade grew into a movement that was soon completely out of his control. In both the Christian east and west, those who had taken the cross began to raise funds for equipment and organize their armies. Recruitment steadily continued, and by the summer of 1096, five large armies had been formed in the west, ready to make their pilgrimage to the Holy Land.

Concurrently, ordinary Christian people—including women and children—were being recruited to a number of other unauthorized and ill-prepared crusading forces. Preachers such as Peter the Hermit, who resided in France, were able to recruit a huge number of willing combatants from all social classes and backgrounds. Promising his followers that God would protect them on this divine mission, Peter led his group, part of what's commonly known as the People's or Peasant's Crusade, to

Constantinople. There were some trained knights in their midst, but overall, the People's Crusade was not fit for battle. When the Crusade crossed the Bosphorus Strait against Emperor Alexius' advice in August 1096, its participants were almost entirely massacred by the Turks.

Led by Godfrey of Bouillon, the Duke of Lower Lorraine and the only German prince to take part in the First Crusade, the first official crusading army set off over land, passing from Rhineland through Hungary without incident. The troops reached Constantinople on December 23, 1096, with almost a full contingency and no major incidents.

The next and largest army was that of Bishop Adhemar of Le Puy, Urban's right-hand man and legate for the Crusade, and Count Raymond IV of Toulouse. This army marched through Lombardy and Dalmatia, across northern Italy and then southwards in Byzantine territory. A further three armies crossed the Adriatic Sea from southern Italy: a force of southern Italian Normans led by Bohemond of Otranto; a force of French Normans organized by Duke Robert of Normandy and Robert of Flanders; and a force led by Hugh of Vermandois, brother of the king of France.

The arrival of tens of thousands of crusading troops in Constantinople posed a number of difficulties for Byzantine Emperor Alexius. Apart from the logistics of providing such necessities as food, water, and law and order to the new arrivals, Alexius had the interests of his empire to take care of. The First Crusade leaders readily agreed to Alexius' demand that they return any former Byzantine lands they may conquer to him, but whether this agreement would be upheld remained to be seen. With oaths taken and Emperor Alexius satisfied, the crusading armies were ferried across the Bosphorus Strait from Constantinople to a military base outside Nicomedia.

As the Crusaders prepared to march on Nicaea, the capital of Turkish Asia Minor, Sultan Kilij-Arslan made an egregious error. Convinced that this army was no more serious than the pious rabble of the People's Crusade, Sultan Kilij-Arslan kept his main army stationed on the eastern frontier. Under-defended, Nicaea fell to the Crusaders on June 19, 1097, and the conquering army advanced into central Anatolia.

Sultan Kilij-Arslan caught up with the Crusaders at Dorylaeum but was unable to defeat them, leaving the route to Syria through Anatolia open. The Crusaders, however, were damaged by this battle and found themselves further weakened by a difficult journey through the Anatolian mountains. Pockets of Armenian Christian resistance in the Taurus mountain range helped the Crusaders finally make it to their destination of Antioch, one of the patriarchal sees of Christianity and a heavily-fortified town. The capture of Antioch was a morale-destroying affair that lasted from October 1097 to June 1098 and saw many Crusaders and Byzantine forces die from starvation and pestilence. Eventually, the Crusaders were able to gain entrance to the town but almost immediately found themselves without supplies and besieged within it.

Against all odds, the Crusaders eventually won victory but not before a number of Crusaders had either died in a devastating epidemic (including Bishop Adhemar of Le Puy, the Crusade's spiritual leader) or lost faith in their Holy War and deserted (including Peter the Hermit). One such deserter made contact with Emperor Alexius of Byzantine and informed him that the siege of Antioch was sure to destroy the Crusaders and that the whole mission was a failure. In response Alexius took his armies, which had been occupying recently conquered western Asia Minor, and fled for Constantinople. When the leaders of the Crusader armies heard of Emperor Alexius' retreat, they saw an opportunity to absolve themselves of the oath they had taken. Now the Crusaders felt free to take possession of any lands they conquered, including Antioch and even Jerusalem.

At this point, the Fatimid Caliphate of Cairo extended an olive branch to the Crusaders and opened up the potential of a military alliance. Although followers of Islam, the Fatimid caliphs were Shia Muslims, and as such, they were the enemies of both the caliphs of Baghdad and the Sunnite Muslim Seljuks. The Crusaders' defeat of Turkish powers in Syria had benefited the Fatimid caliphs who at that time controlled all major ports on the south Syrian coast and, in August 1098, had evicted all Turks from inland Palestine, including Jerusalem. Despite their numbers being drastically depleted and their supplies few, the Crusaders declined the offer and proceeded to lay siege to Jerusalem alone.

Before the Fatimids had time to get their relief army to Jerusalem, the Crusaders managed to breach the city's defensive walls. Once the gate to the city was opened and the Crusaders began to pour in, the Muslim governor surrendered and was allowed to leave. Although there were no longer any Christians living within the city walls of Jerusalem, a number of Jewish families had stayed behind to defend their homes and livelihoods. The Jews and Muslims of Jerusalem fought side by side against the Crusaders and were slaughtered side by side when victory was assured.

Men, women, and children were slaughtered in the streets, and the Crusader leaders went against their promise to uphold the sanctity of the city's mosques as places of sanctuary. Even within the Aqsa Mosque, Jewish and Muslim civilians were killed. After the madness, the Crusaders lay down their weapons and prayed at the Church of the Holy Sepulcher, thanking God for returning Jerusalem to Christian rule for the first time in 450 years.

Chapter Three

Establishing the Crusader States

"'In the temple of Solomon,' wrote the ecstatic cleric Raimundus de Agiles, 'one rode in blood up to the knees and even to the horses bridles, by the just and marvelous judgment of God.'"

—Herbert J. Muller

Many of the Crusaders had joined this ambitious military expedition in the name of pilgrimage. Having completed their journey and prayed at the Church of the Holy Sepulcher, these Crusaders turned around and began the long and arduous journey home. Those who remained were left with the unenviable task of forming some kind of government to rule over the territory the Crusaders had haphazardly conquered.

The leaders of the First Crusade elected Godfrey of Bouillon as advocate of the Holy Sepulcher. As a layman, a person who is not of the cloth, Godfrey took this title as an official defender of church property. With only around 6,000 men left of the 20,000 who survived the Crusade to defend the Holy Land, four large western settlements were formed in Jerusalem, Edessa, Antioch, and Tripoli.

While Godfrey took care of Jerusalem, Edessa was ruled by his brother, Baldwin, who declared himself the Count of Edessa. Godfrey ruled for less than a year, and on his death, Baldwin was summoned back to Jerusalem where he rejected the title of defender and assumed the title of king.

Bohemond became the prince of Antioch and ruled over the Syrian coastline and a few adjoining inland cities. His rule was short-lived as he was captured by Muslims in 1100 and released in 1103, at which time he traveled to Europe to convince Pope Paschal II to organize the disastrous new Crusade. Bohemond's nephew, Tancred, had taken over the role of regent in Antioch and had expanded the territory to include the port at Latakia.

Establishing the state of Tripoli was more difficult. Raymond of Saint-Gilles had begun the siege in 1102 but died three years later having fallen short of his goal. His descendants took over and established the new frontier in 1109. Antioch was vulnerable at both the south and the east, where the strong Muslim cities of Aleppo, Hama, Homs, and Damascus exuded threat. It was impossible to move south, so the Crusaders of Tripoli fortified their eastern frontier with castles, such as Krak de Montreal and Krak des Chevaliers.

Very quickly, this Crusader land had been transformed, not into Byzantine territory or a church state but a feudal kingdom ruled by the leaders of the crusader armies. Each of the three territories, and later the fourth territory of Tripoli, were ruled autonomously, although the counts of Edessa and Antioch did acknowledge the king of Jerusalem as their overlord.

In their first few decades, the two northern Crusader states were separated from Jerusalem by a dangerous band of Muslim-controlled territory. Back on solidly Christian soil, the church had continued to regale its worshippers with tales from the frontlines of the Holy War and had no trouble recruiting new members to the Crusader cause. The church knew that it must secure new territories to protect the fragmented and poorly-defended kingdom of Jerusalem. In 1101 a new Crusade was launched by Pope Paschal II. Three armies entered Asia Minor, and each was systematically destroyed by Turkish forces.

At the start of the twelfth century, the Franks, as Muslims referred to the Crusaders, were desperately short of men to defend their Crusader states and yet Muslim forces were unable to reclaim them. This was primarily due to the deep rivalries between different Muslim sects. The caliphs of Cairo made an effort to recover Jerusalem in 1101, 1102, and 1105, but each time they found themselves beaten back by Frankish forces.

In the earliest years of his rule, the self-styled King Baldwin was able to take control of a number of coastal cities including their all-important ports. With help from the Venetians, Pisans, and Genoans—all of whom were keen to play a role in the flourishing trade of luxury goods in the eastern Mediterranean—the Crusaders had control of the coastline (apart from Ascalon and Tyre) from the year 1112. Now that it was easier than ever to send supplies and pilgrims from the west, the Frankish rulers were able to expand their army and push forward their frontier.

The Franks were able to maintain the upper hand for the next few decades. In 1118, King Baldwin died, and the throne of Jerusalem passed to his cousin, Baldwin of Le Bourg, formerly the Count of Edessa. Under Baldwin II's rule, the Franks took the northern coastal city of Tyne in 1124, with the help of the Venetians. Western shipping could now reach the Holy Land with relative ease.

In 1131, the throne passed to Fulk of Anjou who immediately turned his attention to stabilizing the Crusader states' borders. Muslim forces had recently united under the common cause of their own Holy War (jihad) that promised to remove all Christians from the Holy Land. Zangi, governor of Mosul, had been invited to become the ruler of Aleppo in 1128, and in subsequent years had become a man feared by the Crusaders. Initially, Zangi was coerced by the Byzantine Emperor John II to leave the Franks alone, but by the year 1137, he had reached the end of his patience.

Zangi campaigned twice in Syria over the next seven years in an attempt to capture Antioch but failed. When Emperor John II died in a hunting accident in 1143, Zangi took the opportunity to attack the Franks with full force. In 1144, after an incredibly brief siege, Zangi captured the Crusader state of Edessa. The Crusaders were shocked and horrified, and news of this unexpected loss soon reached the leaders of the church in the west who wasted no time in mounting the Second Crusade.

Chapter Four

The Second Crusade

"Whoever devotedly undertakes and performs this most holy journey . . . shall have the enjoyment of eternal reward from the repayer of all men."

—Pope Eugene III

Now, 49 years after the first plea for willing and able men to join the Crusades, Pope Eugenius III issued a formal Crusade bull. This bull, called *Quantum praedecessores*, emphasized the Crusade as a promise of salvation for anyone who undertook it, no matter how far from grace they had already fallen. King Louis VII of France, his Queen Eleanor of Aquitaine, and the western Emperor Conrad III all took the cross along with many of their vassals.

Again, many simple people were moved by the promise of salvation to join the Crusade, and the church had no problem generating vast armies across western Europe. This crusade, however, would differ significantly from the one that came before it in the attitude of the Byzantine Emperor. Unlike Emperor Alexius Comnenus, Emperor Manuel Comnenus was not at all pleased to learn that a new Crusade was on its way to Constantinople. Manuel was maintaining a complicated alliance with the Germans and Venetians against the Normans and had managed to elicit a truce with the Turkish Sultan of Rum.

The German forces led by Emperor Conrad took the land route to Constantinople and then, ignoring the advice of Emperor Manuel, proceeded towards Anatolia via Nicaea. Conrad's army was almost completely annihilated by the Turks in September 1147 at Dorylaeum, the site of a major victory for the Crusaders during the First Crusade.

The French army led by King Louis VII also reached Constantinople and from there tried to march along the coast to Syria. Along the way, the French troops endured punishing winter conditions, ran short of supplies, and found themselves in almost constant skirmishes with the Turkish. By the time Louis reached Antioch, he had lost the majority of his men.

Antioch was ruled by Prince Raymond, the uncle of Eleanor of Aquitaine. Raymond wanted Louis and Conrad to use their remaining troops and attack Aleppo without delay. News had reached the Crusaders that Zangi's son, Nur ad-Din, had orchestrated a massacre of all Christians living in Edessa. Zangi had been murdered in 1146 and had divided his lands between his heirs. Nur ad-Din took Edessa and Aleppo, and Saif ad-Din took Mosul. For the time being, the state of Edessa was a lost cause.

Louis refused to heed Prince Raymond's wishes and took his men to Jerusalem to visit the holy sites. In Jerusalem, the leaders of the Second Crusade took counsel with the existing Frankish barons, and it was decided that the Crusaders would focus their energy on attacking the Syrian stronghold of Damascus to the south. The invasion was a disaster, and even with an army of 50,000 men, the

Crusaders were easily beaten, bringing the Second Crusade to a bloody and humiliating end. Nur ad-Din attacked Antioch in 1149 and had Prince Raymond killed. He added Damascus to his empire in 1154.

The reaction of the German and French leaders to this devastating defeat could not have been more different. While Conrad headed straight for Constantinople to join Emperor Manuel in his war against Roger of Sicily, Louis went back to France to campaign for a Third Crusade, this time against the Byzantine Empire. This plan came to nothing as the Pope would not condone war with the Byzantines, but the idea that the Byzantine Empire was thwarting the good work of the Crusaders took root.

In the decades following the Second Crusade, the kingdom of Jerusalem was largely unaffected by losses on the northern front. Governed by Baldwin III until 1162 and then by Amalric I until 1174, the kingdom remained in the Crusaders' possession. The only conquest carried out during this era was that of the port of Ascalon. Although the capture of Ascalon extended the kingdom's coastline to the south, its importance was negligible compared to Nur ad-Din's control of a great arc of territory from Mosul to the border of eastern Galilee. An intervention from Emperor Manuel stopped Nur ad-Din from attacking the kingdom of Jerusalem in 1159. Neither of the great powers wanted to engage in a lengthy and costly war, so they made peace before blood was shed with Nur ad-Din agreeing to help Manuel against the Turkish Sultan of Iconium.

Now Nur ad-Din turned his attention to Egypt. News reached King Amalric in Jerusalem that Nur ad-Din had sent his best general, Shirkuh, to invade Egypt, and in response, he sent his own army to meet them. If Nur ad-Din managed to take control of Egypt, his power would be unrivaled. With Amalric's forces in Egypt, Nur ad-Din was free to attack Palestine and managed to capture the fortress of Harim. Still concerned about the backlash from the Byzantine emperor, Nur ad-Din stopped there.

Amalric had come to Egypt's aid and forced Nur ad-Din to withdraw. For this service, the Fatimid caliph had agreed to pay Amalric an annual subsidy and allowed him to build a Frankish garrison in Cairo. But within the year, Amalric tried to impose direct rule on Egypt. The Egyptians turned to Nur ad-Din for help, who sent General Shirkuh to Cairo to take control. Shirkuh was appointed vizier of Egypt by the Caliph but died soon after in 1169. Shirkuh's nephew, Saladin, took over his reign. When it came time to choose a successor to the Fatimid caliph, Saladin divided Levantine Islam by appointing the caliph of Baghdad in his place.

Saladin posed a huge threat to the Crusader states. In 1174, both Nur ad-Din and King Amalric died, creating a regency battle that rocked both the Seljuk-Muslim and Frankish-Christian kingdoms. Nur ad-Din was the first Muslim to unite Damascus and Aleppo. Saladin assumed control of Nur ad-Din's territory on his death but, in theory, acknowledged that he was ruled by both the caliph of Baghdad and Nur ad-Din's rightful successor, As-Salih Ismail al-Malik. Saladin legitimized his position with the people by claiming his only aim was to unite the Muslim people of the east so that they could unleash a Holy War that would remove Christians from the Holy Land once and for all.

The threat of the powerful Saladin loomed large, and Raymond of Tripoli and the new king of Jerusalem, Baldwin IV, disagreed about how best to deal with this threat. Baldwin IV was just 15 years old and as a child had been diagnosed with leprosy. Despite these circumstances, Baldwin proved to be a courageous and effective leader. Over the next eight or nine years, Baldwin succeeded in protecting Jerusalem from Saladin and impeded him from conquering the lands of the Zendig princes. On Baldwin's death in 1185, Raymond of Tripoli came to power as regent for Baldwin's infant nephew and made a fragile truce with Saladin.

In the midst of yet another regency battle that almost descended into civil war in Jerusalem, a Frankish lord broke Raymond of Tripoli's truce with Saladin. Enraged, Saladin proclaimed jihad against the entire Latin kingdom and in 1187 assembled a vast army at Ras al-Mar near Damascus. In turn, the Crusaders were forced to gather the best army they could and confronted Saladin's army at the Horn of Hattin, overlooking the Sea of Galilee on July 4. The Frankish cavalry, which up to this point had almost assured their victory, failed when access to a water supply was cut off.

The Crusader army was completely destroyed. Surviving soldiers were captured and sold into slavery, and 200 Knights Templar and Hospitallers were executed; only the king's life was spared. Following this victory, Saladin was able to subdue the rest of the Crusader states with ease. Putting salt in the Crusaders' wounds, Saladin tore down the relic of the True Cross from the Dome of the Rock and paraded it through the streets. Jerusalem was a Muslim city once more.

Saladin agreed to allow Christians to leave Jerusalem unharmed if they paid a ransom. Those who could not were likely sold into slavery while a handful of Syrian or Greek Christians chose to stay and were later joined by a number of Jews. By 1189 the entirety of the former Crusader states apart from Tyre were in Saladin's hands.

Chapter Five

The Third Crusade

"We, however, place the love of God and His honour above our own and above the acquisition of many regions."

—Richard the Lionheart

News of the fall of the kingdom of Jerusalem and the Crusader states reached the west and was so devastating that on hearing the news Pope Urban III supposedly died of shock. Immediately, the next Pope, Gregory VIII, issued another bull, proposing yet another Crusade. Again the response was enthusiastic. Henry II of England and his son, Richard of Aquitaine, took the cross and joined the cause. Philip II of France, William II of Sicily, and Emperor Frederick Barbarossa also joined the Third Crusade.

Guy of Lusignan, who still considered himself King Guy of Jerusalem, lay siege to the strategic city of Acre in August 1189, before the reinforcement of the Third Crusade had arrived. Both armies could access the sea for supplies, so an arduous two-year stalemate ensued. Forced to keep his troops in the field, Saladin was significantly weakened by the pressure applied by Guy of Lusignan's army. The timing was perfect—if only the Crusaders could make it to Jerusalem in one piece.

Departure from the west was delayed when England and France declared war on each other. Then the death of

Henry II of England led to another delay as Richard the Lionheart was crowned the new king. Once on their way, the English army was delayed once more when Richard took a detour to conquer Cyprus in retaliation for the island's capture of his sister and soon-to-be wife. William II of Sicily died in 1189, and the resulting regency battle forced Sicily to bow out of the endeavor altogether. Emperor Frederick Barbarossa, who was 70 years old in 1189, drowned in the Saleph River and the majority of his army was lost while negotiating passes into Syria.

Philip II and Richard the Lionheart finally reached Acre by sea in 1191, and in just three days they were able to break the deadlock and force the Muslim army to surrender. Philip II left immediately for France, while Richard the Lionheart headed south along the Mediterranean coast. In one decisive battle in Arsuf in September 1191, Richard proved that Saladin's army was no match for the heavily armored English field army and forced Saladin into retreat. Richard was able to take the port town of Jaffa and re-establish Christian dominance of the coastline.

But Richard did not have enough manpower to take the fortified and well-defended city of Jerusalem. Richard tried to advance on Jerusalem twice, but each time the zealously religious English king was forced to retreat. In a huge blow to the crusading forces and Christian supporters in the west, Richard agreed to a truce with Saladin that was to last three years. The truce made a strip of coastal territory from Jaffa to Tyre available to the Franks, meaning pilgrimages from the west could be carried out in relative safety. The main objective of the Third Crusade, to reclaim Jerusalem for Christians, was far from met.

Richard had Guy of Lusignan installed as the lord of Cyprus, the formerly Byzantine-ruled island that Richard had conquered at the start of the Crusade, and then he departed for home. In his absence, Philip II had taken the opportunity to prey on English lands. In contrast to the back-stabbing relationship between Richard the Lionheart of England and Philip II of France, Richard seemed to be on good terms with Saladin, and the truce was upheld.

In 1193, Saladin died, and while his descendants, the Ayyubids, continued to rule over his empire they were unable to organize an army capable of threatening the reclaimed Crusader states. The sultans of Egypt were the official heads of state of Saladin's empire, but each province had its own authority who essentially ruled autonomously. Due to the lack of a clear, central power, war between Syrian provinces was common and what central military the Ayyubids could muster had to be prepared to meet the threat of the Mongol power from the north. Genghis Khan and his Mongol horde had already conquered the lands of Khwarazm, Azerbaijan, and Iconium.

With the Ayyubids otherwise engaged, the truce with the Crusaders continued harmoniously with both sides benefitting from trade and peace. The Crusaders were not in control of Jerusalem but made Acre the center of their new Second Kingdom. Sadly, peace could not last long as in 1198 a new pope, Innocent III, turned the focus back to the Latin east and reinvigorated the people's thirst for a new Crusade.

Chapter Six

The Fourth Crusade

"By heart we believe and by mouth confess the one Church, not of heretics but the Holy Roman, Catholic, and Apostolic Church outside which we believe that no one is saved."

—Pope Innocent III

Theobald III of Champagne held a tournament in 1199, during which a number of French noblemen took the cross. While preparing a new crusading army to depart for Venice where they intended to purchase a Venetian-built fleet of ships, Theobald of Champagne died. His place was taken by Boniface of Montferrat who was auspiciously closely related to Emperor Isaac II Angelus of the Byzantine Empire. Isaac had been deposed by his brother, Alexius, and Isaac's son, unhelpfully also named Alexius, had fled. The young Alexius asked Boniface for his help in reclaiming the Byzantine throne, but Pope Innocent III vetoed the plan.

The Fourth Crusade was led by noblemen who had rarely, if ever, experienced warfare or tried to organize and move a military of any size. Boniface drastically miscalculated the size of his army and ordered a Venetian fleet that far exceeded his need and budget. Unable to pay the Venetians, Boniface became embroiled in yet another sidelining intrigue.

In exchange for the massive expense incurred by the Venetians, the doge of Venice proposed that the Crusaders help the Venetians to capture Zadar, a Christian city led by the king of Hungary. Boniface captured Zadar in November 1202 and reconsidered playing a role in restoring young Alexius as emperor of the Byzantine Empire. In return, Alexius promised to secure a union between the Byzantine church and Rome, send an army of 100,000 troops to assist in the Fourth Crusade, and pay a huge sum of money to both the Crusaders and the Venetians.

The Crusaders arrived in Constantinople in June 1203 and, as promised, toppled Emperor Alexius III and elevated Alexius IV to the throne. However, the new emperor was unwilling or unable to provide the treasures he had promised to the Crusaders. The people of Constantinople, who were already filled with anti-Latin sentiment, turned quickly on Alexius IV and deposed him in a coup in January 1204. The Crusaders now knew they had no chance of claiming their prize, and in April 1204 they defied the Pope and sacked Constantinople.

The 1204 sacking of Constantinople is a stand-out moment in the history of the Crusades for its abandoned ferocity. Considering themselves victims of the treachery of the Byzantine Empire that had distracted them from their pilgrimage to the Holy Lands, the Crusaders forgot their oaths and went on a vile rampage, raping the women of Constantinople, destroying the city, and defiling the many holy sanctuaries.

When order was eventually restored, the imperial domain of Constantinople was divided between Venetian and Frankish noblemen. The city never recovered from the sacking and remained dilapidated and barely-populated as long as Christians were in control of it. The sacking of Constantinople had generated ready cash to continue east, but it had also destroyed the already uneasy relationship between the Christian east and west. The Orthodox east and the Latin west now considered themselves enemies.

Pope Innocent III was disgusted and loudly rebuked the Crusaders' actions in Constantinople, but when news reached the ordinary Christian people of the west, it inspired a fervor for the Crusades not seen since the first capture of Jerusalem. Constantinople was the only major city in the ancient world that had made it to the thirteenth century without being conquered. The Crusaders' victory was viewed by some as a gift from God who was providing the wealth the Crusaders needed to recapture Jerusalem.

Chapter Seven

The Children's Crusade and Crusading Against Christians

"Kill them all, for the Lord knows his own."

—Arnaud Amalric

There was a religious backlash to the Crusaders' unexpected victory that was manifested in the Children's Crusade. Participants and supporters of the Children's Crusade believed that the failures of the organized, militarized Crusade were the result of sin. Only those free from sin and pure of heart could hope to reach the Holy Land and reclaim Jerusalem for the Christians. No particular member of the church called for the Children's Crusade nor condoned it, but it happened anyway—a spontaneous, popular movement that saw its victory as assured.

A young man from Cologne named Nicholas assumed the position of leader of the Children's Crusade. Nicholas led thousands of children, elderly people, and women across the Alps and into Italy. Nicholas assured his followers that when they reached the Mediterranean, God would see to it that the sea would disappear so they could walk on dry land to Palestine. On arrival in Lombardy, Nicholas and his thousands of Crusaders headed for various port towns and awaited their miracle. On August 25, 1212, Nicholas stood at Genoa with a band of dedicated followers and, realizing that no miracle was forthcoming, gave up on their Crusade.

In the early years of the thirteenth century, the outbreak of popular crusading fervor brought on by the capture of Constantinople needed direction. No Fifth Crusade had yet been called, and pious knights and laymen who wanted to take the oath, wear the cross, and claim their Crusade indulgence were desperate for a directive. In 1208, Pope Innocent III answered their call and ordered a holy crusade against the heretics of southern France, known as the Albigensians.

Albigensians practiced Catharism and hailed from the city of Albi in the south of France. Catharism was a belief in dualism, the battle between good and evil. The spirit was held to be good while matter, including the human body, was deemed to be evil. The leaders of the religion were deeply ascetic, and yet Catharism was popular amongst the French nobility. The church had been trying for years to break the will of the Albigensians and to force the Cathar leaders to convert to Catholicism to no avail. Raymond VI of Toulouse was the most powerful baron in the south of France, and it was his support of Catharism that kept the religion going. Raymond, it was thought, was involved in the murder of a papal legate who had sent to investigate the practices of the Albigensians in early 1208. In response, Pope Innocent III sent an army.

The Crusaders captured the Cathar town of Beziers and slaughtered its inhabitants without making a distinction between Christians and heretics. Between 1209 and 1215, the Crusaders captured or forced the surrender of all land between Rhone and the Garonne. Simon, the English lord of Montfort, was confirmed by King Philip II as the leader of the region in 1215, but when the people rebelled, another Crusade was launched. Simon was killed in 1218 in a major uprising, and after continuing the fight for a further six years, his son, Amaury conceded defeat. Those who had ruled southern France before the Crusade reclaimed their land, and the practice of Catharism began again and continued as before.

Chapter Eight
The Fifth and Sixth Crusades

"An army, like a serpent, travels on its belly."

—Frederick II, Holy Roman Emperor

Pope Innocent III had never given up on sending another Crusade to the east and since the sacking of Constantinople had been planning the Fifth Crusade. This time, Innocent was determined to learn from the mistakes of previous endeavors and to keep the organization of the mission within the church. Crusade preachers were released into Europe to recruit soldiers and ordinary men; women and children who were unable to fight were encouraged to take part in the Crusade by praying, fasting, and donating funds.

The Fifth Crusade was launched at the Fourth Lateran Council of 1215. For the first time, the church levied a tax of five percent on the clergy to fund the Holy War, and by 1217 the Crusaders were ready to march. Innocent III died before the Fifth Crusade was in motion, but his successor, Honorius III, took over where he left off. In April 1218 Frisian, German, and Italian Crusaders arrived in Acre where they joined the remnants of an army led prematurely by King Andrew of Hungary to Acre in late 1217.

The army was well-equipped and set about capturing Egypt—the strategy introduced by Richard the Lionheart during the Third Crusade. The Crusaders were able to take the port of Damietta in 1219 after a long siege during which the Muslim powers agreed to a peace treaty that involved the cession of the kingdom of Jerusalem. The Crusaders refused peace and for the next year defended their position at Damietta.

In July 1221, the Crusaders began a disastrous advance on Cairo. At that time of year, the Nile was about to flood its delta and the Crusaders' campsite was dangerously close to the water. The Crusaders became, quite literally, stuck in the mud and were unable to defend themselves against the sultan of Egypt's forces. The Crusaders were forced to surrender in a humiliating defeat—the Fifth Crusade had come to nothing.

Poor leadership, a lack of communication, and ignorance about the hydrogeography of the River Nile caused the Fifth Crusade to go out with a whimper rather than a bang. Still, a scapegoat could be found in the figure of Emperor Frederick II. Frederick had taken the cross in 1215 but had neglected to join the Fifth Crusade. Even ten years after taking the cross when Frederick was married to Isabel II, Queen of Jerusalem, he found reasons not to make the journey to the Holy Land. In 1227, the Pope decided that Frederick was abusing his Crusader status to garner support for domestic disputes and had him excommunicated. The pressure was on. Frederick had to go on Crusade, and he had to be successful in reclaiming Jerusalem for the Christians.

Finally, in 1228, Frederick arrived in Acre. Under its last three monarchs, all of whom were women, the Christian kingdom in the east had been poorly managed by consorts and regents who had neither the knowledge of the area nor the political acumen to rule effectively. Frederick, who held the titles of king of Sicily, Holy Roman Emperor, and rightful king of Jerusalem, managed to achieve what others hadn't—not through military strength, but through political diplomacy.

Al-Kamil, the sultan of Egypt, was on bad terms with his brothers who ruled the various factions of Syria. A civil war broke out, and in return for King Frederick's neutrality, the sultan of Egypt granted him Jerusalem, Bethlehem, and a tract of land that would allow pilgrims from the west to reach the Holy Land by sea. With no bloodshed nor political intrigue necessary, King Frederick II had reclaimed Jerusalem for the Christians and achieved what every Crusader prayed for—all while excommunicated.

The Muslim world was aghast that the sultan had handed over Jerusalem so easily and agreed to no less than a ten-year truce with the Crusaders. What the leaders of the Muslim world didn't know at that time was that they didn't need to do anything to destroy their enemies but sit back and watch. The kingdom of Jerusalem was prevented from being restored to its former power and glory, not by the Muslims, but by the Christians themselves.

Sadly, Frederick's wife had died shortly after giving birth to their son in 1228, just before Frederick left on Crusade. This put Frederick's relationship with the powerful barons of the High Court of Jerusalem in jeopardy. As far as these barons were concerned, Frederick was acting as regent for the infant king, and they had no intention of relinquishing any of their power to him. Frederick himself was a dedicated monarchist who believed that the royal prerogative was second only to the will of God. This view was asserted most famously almost three centuries later by no other than King Henry VIII, who considered his will to be so close to the divine that he formed the Protestant Church to elevate himself above the established clergy.

In 1231, a powerful baron of Jerusalem, John Iberian, refused to acknowledge Frederick II's appointment of a new lieutenant in Jerusalem and civil war ensued. The civil war was a disaster for the Crusaders' interests in the east. The war continued for two years and ended in a divided kingdom with Frederick's lieutenant ruling over Tyre and Jerusalem and the Frankish barons in control of everything else. When Frederick's son Conrad came of age, the barons refused to acknowledge his authority until he came to Acre in person and claimed the city as his own by force. Conrad never did, and the barons retained control.

Chapter Nine

The Seventh and Eighth Crusades

"In prosperity, give thanks to God with humility and fear lest by pride you abuse God's benefits and so offend him."

—King Louis IX of France

Frederick's truce with Sultan Al-Kamil of Egypt came to an end in 1239. The sultan had died only the year before, and the Ayyubid princes were locked in a bitter power struggle to take over the leadership of Egypt. Just as the Christian Crusaders had ruined their chances of expanding the kingdom of Jerusalem by engaging in a civil war, the Muslim Ayyubids now weakened their position by fighting amongst themselves.

In 1239 Theobald of Navarre was able to lead a fairly small contingent of Crusaders to the Holy Land where he restored much of the former kingdom of Jerusalem to the west of Jordan to Frankish rule. An English-led Crusade soon followed and confirmed the new land as part of the Crusader state, but the new sultan of Egypt would not accept this new settlement and in 1244 ordered a sacking of Jerusalem that saw the entire Christian population massacred.

This violent conquest and complete disregard for an agreed settlement could not go unchallenged, and this time, in 1245, it was King Louis IX of France who answered the call to arms. France at the time was in a strong position. Thanks to the Albigensian Crusade, Paris had gained control of Provence, and with the support of his brothers—Alphonse of Poitiers and Charles I of Anjou—Louis was able to collect a sizeable levy on clerical incomes to fund the Seventh Crusade.

Following three years of preparation, Louis left France in August 1248 with his brothers, his wife, and a number of prominent French nobles. These nobles led an army thought to be around 15,000 men strong on a mission to attack Egypt. The Seventh Crusade sailed to Cyprus where it remained until May 1249. Louis IX did not want to launch a campaign to take Egypt in winter, and neither did he seem particularly keen to negotiate with eastern powers. The Latin Empire asked for Louis' help to challenge the Byzantine Empire and the leaders of Antioch asked for his help against the Syrians, but Louis remained focused on taking Egypt.

Initially, Louis' Crusade took Damietta on the Nile with little loss of life on either side. But rather than handing over Damietta to the kingdom of Jerusalem, as the major powers of the Christian west had agreed after the Fourth Crusade, Louis set up his own archbishopric and military base there.

Just like the Fifth Crusade of 1221, Louis' Crusade had not taken into account the changing conditions around the River Nile, and when the river flooded in June, the army found itself grounded for a number of months. In November 1249 Louis' Crusade began to march on Cairo but soon received news that Sultan As-Salih Ayyub of Egypt had died. The sultan's death created confusion in Cairo where dissident factions wrestled for power. Perhaps trying to take advantage of the situation, Robert of Artois led an attack on the Egyptian camp of Gideila, close to the city of Al Mansurah. Rejecting the advice of other, more experienced Crusaders, Robert found himself and his men trapped inside the city. Only a handful of Robert's army survived. Louis arrived soon after the disastrous Battle of Al Mansurah with his main army and lay siege to the city.

For the majority of the Crusaders, the end of the siege only came with their death from starvation or dehydration. Despite the futility of this siege, Louis refused to withdraw to Damietta for months, finally leaving Al Mansurah in March 1250. Muslim forces, now led by Sultan Turan-Shah, As-Salih Ayyub's son, intercepted the army at the Battle of Fariskur and what remained of Louis' army was annihilated.

Louis' agony did not end there as he became gravely ill with dysentery and was ransomed for the sum of 800,000 bezants. While a local doctor eventually cured Louis' dysentery, his imprisonment and ransom meant the loss of Damietta. Louis' wife, who had recently given birth, and a number of French nobles were still in Damietta and now in grave danger. On May 6, 1250, the king's ransom was formally arranged, and Damietta was ceded by treaty back to the sultan of Egypt.

Although Louis had lost everything, he refused to return to France and went instead to Acre where he improved fortifications and tried to negotiate the release of imprisoned Crusaders. Louis' inauguration of a French garrison at Acre, combined with his great suffering, earned him the respect of Christians back in the east, but nevertheless, he returned to France in April 1254 having completely failed in the objective of his Crusade.

Despite the great failure of the Seventh Crusade, King Louis IX's crusading days were not over. In the years following Louis' return to France, the situation in the Muslim states of the east had shifted dramatically. A Mongolian army had managed to take Baghdad in 1258, ousting the powerful and long-standing Abbasid Caliphate. In 1260 Egypt was taken over by a new dynasty known as the Mamluks. The Mamluks were former slave bodyguards of the sultan and had orchestrated a murderous coup to take power. The Mamluks, now led by Sultan Baybars, were fierce fighters and were able to defeat the Mongols at Ayn Jalut in Syria. Both the Mongols and the Mamluks posed a huge threat to the Latin states of the east, and the barons of Acre had no idea how to deal with danger.

Baybars took advantage of a war between Genoa and Venice that devastated the Crusader states' resources and manpower. By 1266 Baybars had managed to capture Galilee, Caesarea, Arsuf, and Haifa. And by 1268 he had taken Antioch. Gone were the days of chivalric warfare and diplomatic negotiation the Crusaders had enjoyed with previous sultans. Baybars massacred the Christian population of every settlement he conquered, whether they were natives or settlers, in league with the Mongols or not.

The west could not ignore this bloodshed, and in March 1267 King Louis IX again took the cross. By July 1270, Louis had organized a large force of Crusaders and set sail from Aigues-Morte bound for the Tunisian coast. A second fleet led by the king of Navarre joined Louis in Tunisia, and together they built a fortified camp at Carthage to await the arrival of Charles of Anjou. Once all of the forces were united, they intended to lay siege to Tunis.

By all accounts Louis' Eight Crusade was an even bigger disaster than the Seventh. While the Crusaders awaited Charles of Anjou's arrival, an epidemic of dysentery struck the troops. Louis' son, John Tristan, who had been born in Damietta while his father was imprisoned and ransomed at the end of the Seventh Crusade, died first. Louis himself followed. Charles of Anjou arrived just after his nephew and brother's deaths and evacuated the remaining Crusaders but not before the English arrived to lend a hand. The English joined the rest of the Crusaders and returned to Sicily where they gathered strength until April 1271 and continued to Acre, a journey that became known as the Ninth Crusade.

Chapter Ten

The Last Crusade

"The greatest happiness is to vanquish your enemies, to chase them before you, to rob them of their wealth, to see those dear to them bathed in tears, to clasp to your bosom their wives and daughters."

—Genghis Khan

Prince Edward had only 1,000 men under his command when he arrived in Tunis but his army, combined with that of Charles of Anjou and the English forces, immediately set sail for Acre. Having such a small number of Crusaders, Edward and Charles had to put strategy first and began their campaign with a series of raids. First they took Nazareth, and then they took the town of Qaqun. The Ninth Crusade arrived in Acre just in time to repel an attack from Baybars, who avoided a lengthy and likely fruitless siege with a prompt withdrawal.

Edward wisely sought co-operation with the Mongols, the greatest threat to the Muslims. In September 1271 Edward received agreement from the Mongol ruler Abagha that the Crusaders and Mongols would join forces for a concerted attack on Baybars' army. The following month, Mongol invaders conquered Aleppo and marched southwards, triggering a mass exodus of Muslim populations who were not ignorant of the Mongols' reputation for bloodlust. Baybars launched a counter-attack in early November by which time the Mongols had already retreated of their own free will, rich with the spoils of war.

Baybars decided a change of tack was needed and built a sizeable fleet in order to attack Cyprus, drawing Cypriot forces out of Acre and increasing his chances of defeating what remained of Edward's army. This plan failed when Baybars' fleet was destroyed off the coast of Limassol. Edward made a valiant effort to unite the warring factions within the Christian state and was successful in negotiating a truce with Baybars, agreed to last ten years, ten months, and ten days.

But just one month later, an assassination attempt was made on Edward who miraculously survived. Edward fled to Sicily to recover and received the news in November 1272 that his father had died. Edward finally returned to England in the summer of 1274 where he was crowned the king of England.

After the Ninth Crusade, the Crusader kingdom continued to spiral downward into total collapse. Insurmountable differences and rivalries between the different Christian powers in the Crusader states made a united Latin east impossible to achieve. The Genoese and Venetians were constantly at each other's throats; absentee monarchs were unable to wrest authority from barons of Jerusalem; immigration had completely ceased due to the frightening death toll, and support for the Crusades in the west dwindled to nothing.

The vulnerability of the Crusader states was sensed by the Mamluk Sultan Qalawun who had defeated the Mongols in 1281. Throughout the 1280s, the Mamluks systematically destroyed what remained of the truce put in place by Prince Edward of England. Christian pilgrims were persecuted more than ever before, and the Mamluks demanded an ever-increasing sum of tribute from the kingdom of Acre.

In 1289 Tripoli fell to Sultan Qalawun. While Qalawun was victorious in the attack on Tripoli, his army was diminished by the effort, and Qalawun lost his eldest son in the fighting. Taking two years to rebuild his army, Qalawun went on to conquer Acre in 1291. The pretext for Qalawun's invasion of Acre centered on the murder of 19 Muslim merchants by Christian pilgrims. The pilgrims had supposedly attacked in retaliation for a previous attack on them, but the details are not clear. Diplomatic relations between the two sides broke down, and Qalawun took his opportunity to seize the last Crusader state in the Holy Land. All survivors of the Acre massacre were enslaved, and the Crusaders' many fortified castles were systematically destroyed.

Sultan Qalawun died during the siege of Acre and his son, Khalil, took over his sultanship. What remained of Crusader power in the east retreated offshore to the island of Cyprus, and the Mamluk Muslims focused on the very real threat presented by the Mongols. The Crusades were officially over, 208 years after they first begun.

Conclusion

The Crusades may have officially come to an end with the taking of Acre in 1291, but in many parts of Europe, the crusading spirit showed no signs of dying out. Successive Popes tried to organize aid for the remaining few Christians in the east and even made tentative calls to Crusade again, which were met with little response. As England and France were entering the period of the Middle Ages when their relationship became so poisonous that it resulted in the Hundred Years' War, the main crusading powers were in no position to take the cross.

The Knights Hospitaller of Jerusalem managed to take the now Greek island of Rhodes in 1308 and maintain a headquarters there before moving on to Smyrna where they remained until 1402. Still, there was no real attempt to take control of mainland territory, and Cyprus remained the only Crusader outpost in the east.

The Ottoman Turks were able to enter Europe for the first time in 1348, thanks to a Byzantine civil war that left Constantinople vulnerable. The Turks took Bulgaria, most of Greece, and stood knocking at the door of Constantinople. Now Crusader rhetoric focused not on recapturing Jerusalem but on defending Christian Europe itself. They feared that the powerful Turks would advance in central and western Europe, and it was only when the Latin and Greek Christian churches reunited and worked together that the Christian west was able to push back against the Muslim east. It wasn't until the late fifteenth century that the Spanish Reconquista was able to reclaim

Christian territory and expel Muslims from Europe altogether.

It would be nice to think that from the sixteenth century onwards tension between the Christian west and Muslim east dispersed and their turbulent history was forgotten, but that is not the case. The rise of Protestantism in the west was both a catalyst for and a result of the demise of the Crusades. Crusading smacked of Catholic indulgence and became yet another argument against the authority of the clergy. This massive split in the Christian church led to wars between and within Christian nations that took the focus off the Muslim threat. From the Reformation right up to the age of Louis XIV, crusading never disappeared from the public consciousness and arguments were constantly put forth to launch yet another Crusade.

Even centuries after the last unsuccessful Crusade, the Crusades had a lasting impact on medieval Europe. The kingdom of Jerusalem was essentially Europe's first colony and inspired later monarchs and military leaders to embark on massive projects of colonization. The behavior of both crusading forces and their often backstabbing leaders led to a split between the Orthodox east and Latin west that would never heal. On a more positive slant, the Crusades created lasting trade between the Christian and Islamic worlds, and the cultural exchange is thought to have been a major factor in the European Renaissance. By the Romantic era, the reality of the Crusades was forgotten and, in England and France in particular, the Crusades came to embody the very notion of chivalry.

How much the Crusades were an aggressive act of Christian fanaticism and how much they were a defensive military intended to check the spread of Islam and reclaim Christian territory is still debated. What cannot be debated is that 1.7 million ordinary people, both Christian and Muslim, died as a result of the Crusades, and that loss of life cannot be considered chivalric in the slightest.

Made in the USA
Monee, IL
16 September 2023

42871235R00026